RETURNING THE SERVE INTELLIGENTLY

RETURNING THE SERVE INTELLIGENTLY

by Sterling Lord

UNITED STATES TENNIS ASSOCIATION

INSTRUCTIONAL SERIES

Illustrations by George Janes

DOUBLEDAY & COMPANY, INC.
GARDEN CITY, NEW YORK
1976

Library of Congress Cataloging in Publication Data
Lord, Sterling, 1920–
Returning the serve intelligently.
(Instructional series)
1. Tennis.   I. Title.   II. Series.
GV995.L62   796.34'22
ISBN: 0-385-05297-9
Library of Congress Catalog Card Number 73–20532

Contents

Introduction

This book is intended only for tennis players interested in improving their games. It is not for you if you are or were a nationally ranked player; you should know it all by now. It is also not for you if you haven't yet started to think—even a little bit—about how to outmaneuver your opponent. If your game hasn't reached that level, then you probably don't know enough tennis to benefit from this book.

If, on the other hand, you are looking for ways to beat the man or woman you have been losing to every Saturday morning; or to help you and your partner win the club doubles championship this year; or to improve the quality of your own doubles play so you will be the player everyone seeks out as a partner, then this is the book for you.

There is no other book extant devoted solely to how to return the serve in tennis. What you find here are pieces of information and intelligence as well as plans of play that the author has learned by watching and listening to coaches and nationally ranked players, or learned himself by deduction and analysis during almost half a century of play—from the days of Bill Tilden to the days of Jimmy Connors—on tennis courts across the United States.

This book can also enable you to remove the tyranny of that one player you know you should beat, but never can

—the player whose game is inferior to yours in all departments but one, yet he can still beat you—because he has an overpowering serve!

RETURNING THE SERVE INTELLIGENTLY

I like to think that God is with me, but when it's 5–4 and my serve, I can go it alone.

Richard "Pancho" Gonzales

I

An Examination of the Potential

Most players approach the return of service negatively. The serve is, after all, designed to give the advantage to the server; it is the one stroke in tennis a player can hit from a standing position—that is, without being on the run—and where he has total control of the position of the ball. It is also the one stroke a player can practice endlessly without an opponent. Therefore the server theoretically has an enormous advantage as he serves.

These are the thoughts that run through the receiver's mind as he steps up to receive service. No wonder he approaches it with a lack of confidence. "If I can just reach the serve and keep the ball in play," he tells himself, "I have a small prayer of a chance at the point."

Normally, only the tournament-hardened player can avoid thoughts and worries such as these as he awaits his opponent's serve.

Let me suggest a better way of approaching the receiving game. Think of it this way: your opponent (the server) is committed to hit from one spot on his court—and it is a spot you can see and determine many seconds before he hits the ball—so you know where he is and where he will be hitting from. He doesn't know where you will be. He only knows where you are standing at the moment he starts his serving motion. After that moment, he is committed but you aren't. You have a few extra seconds (probably two to three seconds until he hits the ball, and perhaps two or three more from the time he hits the ball until it reaches you) to change your position. You can do a great deal on a tennis court in five seconds.

Furthermore, if you have been studying your opponent's serve (either scouting it before the match or observing him as he serves to you), you can get a pretty good idea of where he is going to hit the ball—before the ball reaches your court. (I will explain this in some detail in a later chapter.)

Also, in good tennis (and this is truer as the tennis gets better) the server knows he has to win his serve each time in order to win the match. Pressure varies during the course of a match, of course, but there are many instances where the pressure is much greater on the server than on the receiver.

In 1974, Roscoe Tanner, the young left-hander from Lookout Mountain, Tennessee, had just upset Ilie Nastase in five sets at Forest Hills. "Coming from behind isn't as difficult as you think," Tanner was quoted as saying. "You need only one service break a set to win."

Now that you see it is possible to approach the return of service in a positive frame of mind, let's structure the details of your mental approach to receiving service.

In the first place, it is possible to hit either an offensive or a defensive shot off your opponent's serve, and the choice of which kind of shot you hit is not always determined solely by his serve.

Returning the serve offensively, which is not always possible, has the added advantage of neutralizing the effect of the serve. In trying for an offensive or aggressive

At this point in his swing, the server has already committed himself, but you—the receiver—can start to move.

return of service, you increase your own chances of error, but you also put additional pressure on your opponent, a pressure that is most likely going to result in an increased number of double faults, and certainly will result in his missing a greater percentage of first serves. It is obviously easier for you to hit offensively off your opponent's second serve than off his first.

With all this talk about returning serve offensively, what do we mean by the term, and how, from a technical point of view, is it accomplished?

Returning a serve offensively involves an effort on the part of the receiver to place the server in the position of greatest possible disadvantage. Returning service for a placement ace is obviously an offensive return; so is one that forces the server to run hard to retrieve it, or forces him to hit the ball when he is off balance, or in any way to return the ball in a manner that allows you to attack or to force or control the play.

Despite what I have written on previous pages, the primary function of the service return is to get the ball in play. Hitting the ball offensively should not be contemplated until you have the fundamentals of service return firmly in hand, and until your ground strokes are well honed. It should probably be done with great discretion. The service return is, after all, only a ground stroke hit under more difficult conditions than you are hitting during a rally.

Speaking only of singles, for the moment, you can deduce very quickly the possibilities for directing your return. If your opponent is following his serve to the net, you will be trying to (1) pass him on either side as he comes in, (2) hit to his feet (probably a spin shot) so he

Returning the serve offensively can put additional pressure on your opponent and neutralize the supposed advantage of a strong serve.

is forced to err or to hit up, or (3) lob, hopefully over his head. Your choice will obviously be with whatever shot you are hitting best against this particular opponent, keeping in mind that surprise—mixing up your shots—is an additional weapon you should not ignore.

If your opponent is not coming to the net, or not coming in regularly, then your object should be to hit as deeply as possible to his weaker side. If he has no apparent weaker side, you might hit your return in the direction that will make your opponent run the farthest, or—thinking ahead to his next shot—hit to the side or in the manner that will make him return the ball to your best shot, or to your specific shot that can score against him.

But the fundamental mission on return of serve is to put the ball in play. It is a matter of judgment—your personal evaluation, courage, and temperament—as to how aggressive you want to be as you return the service.

II

The Necessary Technical Equipment

The serve presents a unique problem to the receiver. The ball approaches him from a different angle and with different spins on it than any other shot hit at him during the game—with the possible exception of some overhead smashes. The serve is hit at him from a higher altitude and perhaps with greater force than most ground strokes. In many cases it carries a sidespin or element of slice that is never characteristic of a forehand or a backhand drive, since the slice on a forehand or backhand will only alter the height and length of the bounce, rarely its direction.

These unique elements demand greater concentration on your part as you receive. They not only require watching the ball carefully, but also demand that you focus on *a spot in the center of the ball*. Focus on this spot, and keep watching it until you can actually see the ball meet the strings of the racket. Try to keep your eyes on that spot on the ball until the strings compress the ball. Most players—even the best tournament players—tend not to watch the ball after it comes within three or four feet of its point of contact with their racket.

If you focus so long on the ball, you may wonder, how can you tell where your opponent is on the court? Is he rushing the net? Is he moving over to his backhand anticipating a return there? Basically, you have two ways of making this determination: (1) if you have been observant of him and his game you should know his habits, and (2) as you are starting to move toward his serve to make your return, he has come into your line of vision so that you know what he is starting to do, or where he is just a few seconds before you actually hit your return.

A second essential to effective returning is to bend over or crouch low as you await the serve. It is much more important to do this while receiving serve than while awaiting ground strokes. The crouch serves the vital purpose of bringing your eyes closer to the plane of flight of the ball. You can detect differences in speed and in direction and in spin of the ball much more readily from this position. In addition, of course, you can start toward the ball more rapidly from a crouching position. You are simulating the crouch of a runner at the start of a race. There is no effective returner of serve in the game of tennis who does not receive serve from a crouched position.

Third, as you hit the ball, you must make every effort— and this is more important on service return than on any other shot—to move your weight or your body *through* the ball. (This applies on every return except a lob or a soft dink you direct at the feet of the net-rushing server.) You must move your body, your weight, or at the very least the upper part of your body (chest and shoulders) forward or toward the net or in the direction in which you are hitting the ball. This gives the service return distance and power and is much more reliable in accomplishing these ends than the use of arm motion alone. If your opponent's serve is weak enough or your returning ability strong enough so you can move into the net on your return, then the motion of your body as you move toward the net will, of course, move your weight through the ball.

A word about the grip: there is no absolute answer to this question. You can receive service using your back-

hand grip, or receive using your forehand grip, without attempting to change your grip as you prepare the stroke (even though the ball comes to your so-called wrong side). Or you can use a grip midway between your normal forehand and backhand grips, again not changing before you hit the ball. Finally, you can stand ready to receive using any one of the three grips above, but change to the appropriate grip (forehand grip if it comes to *your* forehand, etc.) as you prepare to hit the ball. This can only be done if you are playing relatively deep in the court; you will not have time if you are standing in close, trying to take the ball on the rise.

Tony Trabert, formerly two-time winner of the U. S. National Championships at Forest Hills, recommends receiving service holding the racket as you would for your weaker return. In other words, if your backhand is weaker than your forehand, await service with your backhand grip. On the other hand, Jan Kodes, the Czechoslovakian star and ranked No. 7 in the world at the end of the 1973 season, recommends awaiting serve using the grip of your stronger side.

A good tournament player, who can anticipate well the nature and direction of a serve coming toward him, will probably always shift his grip so that he has the appropriate grip by the time he hits the ball. As he stands or crouches awaiting the serve, his nonhitting hand is holding his racket lightly at the throat. This helps him shift the grip quickly and easily.

Against players of lesser strength, it may not be necessary to shift your racket as you hit the service return; you may be able to return it perfectly well—and, as a matter of fact, be more consistent with your returns—if you hit with the composite grip with which you have been awaiting the ball.

The solution for you will come from trial and experimentation until you arrive at the grip that will allow you to return service effectively and consistently. Incidentally, holding the racket at the throat with the other hand also makes it possible to get the racket back quickly. Getting it back too slowly is a common cause of error in service return.

The final general area to consider in your effort to maximize your effectiveness in returning service is your position on the court. Let's talk first about singles. Against a player whose serve lacks versatility, you can place yourself on the court in a manner to cover the spot or side of the service court you know he serves most effectively into, leaving open the area he has most trouble hitting. This puts extra pressure on the server, of course.

A second way of handling this type of server is to leave slightly open the area you know he likes best to serve into, then move over to cover that area as he throws up the ball and starts his serving motion—in other words, in the first instant he has committed himself and can no longer change the direction or nature of the serve. Then, presumably because you are already in the spot ahead of his serve, you should be able to hit an effective, offensive return.

How far forward or how far back you stand to receive service is again a matter of your own confidence and judgment. Many world-class players advocate standing *on* the baseline to receive the first service, with your outside foot on the singles sidelines. It depends upon how well you can handle your opponent's serve. Can you handle it well enough to keep him from coming in to the net behind his own serve? Are you having trouble keeping him from coming to the net, even though you are returning his serve consistently? If so, perhaps you should be standing in closer to receive. If you are in closer, possibly close enough to hit the serve on the rise, your swing is necessarily short. You are not quite blocking the ball, but you don't have time for the leisure of a long backswing or follow-through. Your power comes from the speed of your opponent's serve, plus the forward motion of your own body as you move toward the net. The effectiveness of this return depends upon perfect timing; upon catching the server by surprise or off balance because of the quickness of your return; and upon accuracy in terms of your own placement of the shot. Topspin or underspin cannot be an element of this kind of return.

You can also return effectively and offensively from a position a foot or two behind the baseline. From this position, however, you not only have the time but also must take the time and the effort to swing fully. And spin is almost essential to your shot. If your opponent is following his serve into the net, a soft underspin shot at his feet or a heavily topped drive increase your effectiveness enormously. If hit well, such a return will force the net-rushing server to hit up or hit weakly, or both.

Your choice of where you stand to receive service should result from your analysis of your own ability to receive your opponent's serve in general; your opponent's position vis-à-vis the sun; your analysis of both his state of fatigue and your own; and the surface of the court. A clay court slows down a serve, of course; a wood surface or hard outdoor surface usually produces a fast, skidding ball. On a fast surface, the server's potential against you is greater as he serves toward the alleys, where the fast skid will mean that the ball is skidding away from you. Against a versatile server, therefore, you should probably leave a slightly larger opening down the middle, both in

Your receiving position is a product of your opponent's position on the court; the court surface; fatigue—his and yours—and your previous ability, in the match, to play his serve well.

the deuce and the ad courts.

Flexibility through the duration of a match is extremely important in service return. Factors change as a match progresses. Your opponent may tire, he may be unsettled by your good play; you may have forced him to try serves that are low-percentage shots for him; or his concentration may be poorer, erratic, or nonexistent as the match progresses. Most players, short of the tournament-hardened tennis player, are not concentrating as effectively after they've served three or four games as they were at the start of play. In addition, many players go to sleep, in effect, during a match; they may have stopped all creative thinking the minute the first bit of physical fatigue sets in. This is the player against whom you should change tactics during the match. Sometimes you have to be careful not to change so severely that you wake him up. If you are winning, and the margin of your winning is not diminishing, then you would be foolish to change. But if you are losing, or your lead is slipping, then change might be a good idea. Move in closer, or back farther; or stand farther to one side; or lob occasionally instead of driving your return—anything to try to break up the concentration and game of your opponent.

III

Anticipating the Direction of Your Opponent's Serve

If you can determine before your opponent serves the ball just where or approximately where it will go, you have a great advantage: you can start moving in that direction before the ball leaves the server's racket; you will have plenty of time to prepare your own stroke; you can increase your chances of hitting an effective return of service; and you begin to demoralize or upset the server.

Anticipation is a marvelous weapon on the tennis court. Most, but not all, great champions have it. Anticipation is composed of your analysis of the percentages plus your reading of your opponent's stroke habits. By analyzing the percentages I mean that given the score; given the server's pattern of serves in the match thus far; given his state of fatigue and general level of tennis intelligence, you should have a fairly good idea of the nature of the serve that is about to come at you.

There are other percentage factors—for example, is he experienced enough to know that in a pressure point your backhand may provide a more reliable return of service than your forehand? In most cases with players of a middle level, this is true (particularly if the receiver is tired or nervous) because the receiver has to work harder, to move his feet farther and quicker, to get in position for the return on his forehand. Is the server experienced enough to know how tired you are, and to know if you are likely to adjust instantly to a different kind of serve?

The second element of anticipation, reading your opponent's habits, involves prior study as well as observation during the match. The variables for the server are: (1) his position at the baseline, (2) his stance—whether he is standing fully sideways or only partially sideways to the net, (3) how high he throws the ball, and finally (4) where he tosses the ball in relation to the body.

The last point is the most important sign you can read. If he tosses the ball back over his head, the chances are that he will serve you a heavily top-spinning ball like Tom Gorman, the American internationalist, often does on his second serve. If he throws the ball far out to his right—and in this paragraph I am assuming that the server is right-handed—then the serve will inevitably be a slice, which will bounce to the right. If the server's toss is a little less far to the right, it will be flatter, probably faster.

As you try to read your opponent's toss, don't forget that depth—or how far he leans into the court—is another factor you should try to read. Just how the lean relates to direction of serve you can only tell after studying the server in action a number of times. One general rule here is to move slightly in the opposite direction from the server's toss: If he tosses to his right, he will probably hit to your right, and vice versa.

The final factor for the receiver to consider falls into the area between anticipation and observation: How deep in the court is your opponent's serve? A receiver playing deep for a hard or deep service can be caught off balance if he does not notice and immediately take advantage of a short service coming to him. Failure to notice and respond to the short service not only means you have failed to take advantage of a short ball, but it often means you will miss the ball, either making an outright error or setting it up for the server's follow-up shot.

After his 1974 victory over Ilie Nastase at Forest Hills, where he came from two sets down, Roscoe Tanner was quoted as saying, "Nastase was standing far back for the serve, waiting to give it his best shot. So I began to hit a sliced serve, rather softly, to make him reach for it and bend over on the soft grass. It worked, I think."

Tennis, like many other sports, requires of the player certain physical effort as well as certain mental effort. The proportion varies from sport to sport and from player to player. This section on anticipation may seem to put too much emphasis on thought, or the mental aspect of the game, to the extent that the receiver could become so involved and confused he might not have time or energy to fulfill the primary requirement: Get the ball back over the net.

It was J. F. "Curly" Thomason, brilliant, firebrand Burlington, Iowa, high school basketball coach in the 1930s who said, "Too much thinking spoils the team."

Obviously, it is difficult to fill your head with all the factors mentioned during a serve, or while waiting for a serve, but after study and practice most of these principles will become automatic with a serious, good player. Or you can use them as checkpoints when you are in trouble.

IV

Handling the Second Serve

Your opponent's second serve will almost inevitably be slower than his first serve. It may also be shorter, and there may be more spin on the ball than on the first serve. Most players who are serious about their game will have been taught to hit the second serve not as hard as the first, and to put more spin on it—probably topspin (this is traditionally known as the American Twist)—because spin will enable the server to better control the ball. A

spinning serve is also more difficult for you to return than a flat, spinless ball.

Exactly how you alter your return techniques from first to second serve depends primarily upon how weak your opponent's second serve is, or how readily you feel you can take advantage of that serve. There is greater pressure on the second serve since the server knows he must get this one into the court in order to have a chance of winning the point. He has lost the freedom or breadth of opportunity that the first serve gives him.

The chances are that you should step forward or move forward to receive the second serve anywhere from a foot or two to five or six feet. Don't take up all the slack because you may want to be moving forward through the ball on the way to the net, and you can hit the ball better and move forward more quickly from a running start, as opposed to a standing start.

Another reason for not moving in too close while awaiting the second serve is that you may have greater opportunity or desire to run around the second serve to take it on your forehand, and to do this you need adequate space.

When your opponent has an effective, heavily spinning second serve, you have different choices to make, of course. A high-spinning second serve to your backhand may drive you back or keep you back. Against such a serve, you should receive in the same position as your receiving position for the first serve; or you may want to move in close, to try to take it on the rise before it kicks up and out, and to block it back. This can be an effective idea, particularly if your opponent is following his serve to the net.

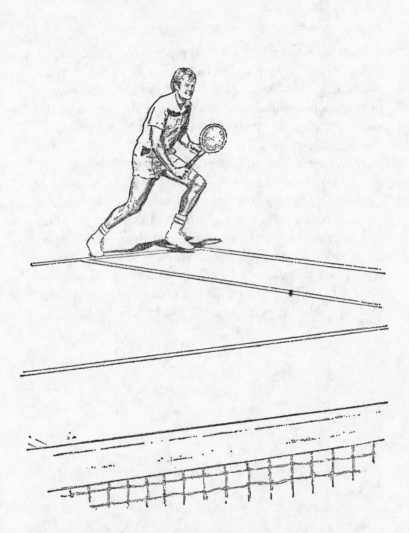

If your opponent can hit a high-spinning second serve to your backhand, you may have to receive in the same position you would use for receiving his first serve.

Sometimes the server's second serve is so soft and at the same time without spin that the receiver can easily err by overhitting, or by taking his eye off the ball. The way to handle such a soft shot is to use the body more and the arm less; use a much shorter backswing than you would normally, keep your eye on a spot in the center of the ball, and move forward through the ball on the way to the net. Where you hit such a ball depends upon the opportunities available on that particular point, but such a serve in singles brings up the drop shot as a possible alternate service return. A server with such a weak second serve, which you have been returning deep and effectively, will naturally fall back after serving. If you are alert to his falling back on his heels, or away from the net, that should be the perfect moment to hit a drop shot.

V

The Strategy of Variety

Throughout this book I have frequently mentioned change, or variety in returning service. It is an important weapon in all aspects of tennis. Often the player who has had considerable professional instruction but minimal tournament or match-play experience can hit an individual stroke beautifully and effectively, but can't maintain that level of shot performance in serious play. He looks amazingly impressive in practice, so let's call him Johnny Hotshot. One of the aspects of his game he probably has not developed is his footwork. Developing good footwork takes long hours of hard work, much of it very tedious.

He must have good footwork to enable him to adjust from one shot to another, so you should be trying to hit him shots that make him work, that don't allow him to hit the textbook shot. One way to do this, to test the game of Johnny Hotshot, is to put spin on your shot—either topspin or underspin. A teaching pro will have been hitting him balls with no spin on them, in order to give Johnny maximum opportunity to return them. You are trying to give him minimal opportunity to return.

Second, make him stretch for the ball. Chase him from side to side, or bring him up, then send him racing back under a lob. By the time you have done this on a point, or two, or three, the dynamics of the match will have changed, you will have discovered a great deal about his game (and he about yours), and you may be in the driver's seat.

The case I've just described illustrates a point applicable to return of service as well, of course. Changing or altering your return of service to throw him off guard and to test him may well break up his stroke pattern. Here's another very good method of disconcerting Johnny Hotshot: if you know, for example, that his best serve is a hard, flat service near the center in the ad court, then try leaving that area slightly exposed as you await service. You will have to judge how far to leave it exposed; what you are trying to do is to let him notice the opening, but keep him from thinking you are purposely leaving it open (you can't afford to let him think that, or the ploy may not work). Then, as he throws up the ball, you move over to cover the spot so you are ready and present when the serve reaches you. Giving your opponent an opening to hit his best shot, then getting it and hitting it back effectively, or even for a winner, is one sure way to demoralize a player who has very little match-play experience.

VI

Taking a Lesson from Nastase

Supposing your opponent is left-handed, you are right-handed, and he is serving to you in the ad court. You are playing singles. The most obvious shot for him to hit is a slice serve to your backhand. If he takes the other alternative and tries to hit the ball into the corner of the service court near the center service line (meaning on your forehand), his chance of error is greater. And further, a down-the-middle shot like that will have pulled you (the receiver) into perfect position to encounter the next shot, meaning that you are now in the center of the court, near the baseline, and fully prepared (as far as position is concerned) for his next return.

So we now have at least two reasons the server should not or will not try serving to your forehand, as you stand in the ad court. In addition, serving to your backhand is probably an easier and more natural shot for him, since most players tend not to turn their body and shoulders far enough around in the direction of their serving arm when they serve, thus drawing the serve off to their opposite side—the side away from their serving arm—or in this case, your backhand.

All right, those are the odds and the givens. I have said that the receiver needn't always be at the mercy of the server, so what can you now do? Well, one thing you can do is to receive service standing far to the left, with both feet out in the alley, and even farther out than that if you can get by with it. What have you accomplished? First, you've undoubtedly rattled your opponent. Second, you have put pressure on his serve. More than likely he will either try to serve farther to your left, or he will be forced to try to serve down the center line, where the percent-

ages for him are poor. If he does try down the center line, you should be able to guess where it is coming by observing the slightly different manner in which he tosses the ball for the serve, or places his feet, or leans his body as he stretches to hit the ball.

But you have to think it out through one additional step to really take advantage of this maneuver. You have put pressure on your opponent, you have forced him to try for serves he normally doesn't try for, but he still serves the ball in the court. Assuming the percentages have worked for you, he may well have missed his first serve and hit his second serve in court. Already you have an advantage because his second serve is weaker than his first. What you now have to do is to hit your return offensively, to turn your partial advantage into a full advantage and eventually the point.

I am not going to describe all the possible service returns from this position. They are not infinite, though they are numerous. The crucial return from this position, the one potential big winner, is a forehand hard down the line. That is one extra shot you have added to your repertoire in this particular situation, by standing far out in the alley to receive service. A note of caution: you must be sure of hitting a winner before you try it, because if you hit it less than brilliantly, your opponent has a huge open area—your forehand side—in which to return the ball.

"Well," you say, "this is fine for left-handers who can't hit the center corner, but what about the other 95 per

cent of the tennis players in this world?"

The answer is that this technique will work against any player, right-handed or left-handed, who can't easily hit the center corner on the ad court. It is the very technique used often by Ilie Nastase, and was particularly effective when he beat Australian Fred Stolle in a stadium match in the quarterfinals of the USLTA Open Championships at Forest Hills in 1972. Nastase gave Stolle plenty of room down the center, but even this seasoned international player couldn't score, and on grass, where service has an even greater advantage than on clay. Nastase won, 6–4, 3–6, 6–3, 6–2. Both those players are, of course, right-handed.

One final note about the use of this technique: no strategy is necessarily going to work the first time. If it doesn't work against a certain opponent you feel should be bothered by it, try to observe his serving motion and court manner to see if it is putting pressure on him even though he is not yet missing. If it isn't, you have either misjudged your man, or are not executing your move effectively. Change or variety is another good strategy, as I've mentioned previously, so perhaps you shouldn't use the technique each time you receive in the ad court. You have to be the judge of when and how often to use it. In addition, most players who are not tournament-hardened serve better at the start of the match. They are less tired. As the match wears on they become more fatigued and thus find it more difficult to concentrate. Perhaps you should wait until near the end of the first set, or even into the second set before trying this strategy. When to use it is something you can only learn from experience, and should be based on your perceptions of your opponent's game, of his mental or emotional condition, and of his physical condition.

The above presupposes an attempt at an offensive return of service. There is no point to the maneuver if you intend to return the serve defensively.

VII

A Completely Different Game— Returning Service in Doubles

Though a good serve limits the options of the receiver in singles, that limitation is mild compared to what happens to you when you are receiving the same serve in doubles. You have one advantage only over singles: you know the chances are much greater than they are in singles that your opponent will follow his serve into the net. Your disadvantage is that you have only about 60 per cent of the space in which to return service, since the server's partner is standing at the net potentially blocking you from hitting down the line, and ready to dash across the net to intercept and put away any weak return you might hit to the server.

Far and away the best return of service in doubles is a spin shot hit low and crosscourt to the feet of the net-rushing server. It should be hit low enough and fast enough to keep the netman (the server's partner) from intercepting it, or poaching. If it is effective, it will force the server to hit his return high enough (this is called hitting up) so that either you or your partner can move in and volley the ball away for a placement and point.

Let's suppose you are receiving service in the deuce court. (This is often and incorrectly called the forehand court. Incorrectly, because the player with the stronger forehand should probably, on a doubles team, have that forehand available to cover the middle of the court—as

would a right-handed player who played the ad court. Down the middle is where many key volleys and ground strokes are hit in good doubles.) For a right-handed player, playing against right-handed players, the deuce court is a more difficult court in which to receive than the ad court, for two reasons: (1) Returning a service hit well

to your backhand forces you to hit at an obtuse angle—
meaning you will be hitting it farther to your left than the
angle at which the ball has come to you—and with your
back to the net. In such a shot the use of any speed and
the exertion of any real control are extremely difficult.
(2) The server's partner (the netman) can more readily
poach on your return, since in poaching from his deuce-
point position he is poaching with his forehand and thus
is able to start quicker and reach farther than if he is trying to poach from his ad-point position.

Incidentally, usually the poorer player of the two plays
the deuce court. Why? Well, for one thing, the key points
are more frequently played in, or commence with a serve
in, the ad court. Also, just in terms of percentages, the
receiver has a greater opportunity, a better crack at con-
trolling the point, from the ad court. A strong player receiving in the ad court, directing and/or acting in concert
with his partner, can maneuver or manipulate his opponents so that they are scrambling and hitting up much of
the time. If the partners are of equal strength, usually the
steadier of the two plays the deuce court.

Now, back to you, receiving in the deuce court, now
that you know how difficult it is. Your mission is to keep
the netman from poaching, to keep the server from coming in as fast as he wants to, and to keep the ball low so
that neither opponent can hit an offensive or point-win-
ning volley off your return. This will, hopefully, enable
you to attain the net beside your partner and to force
your opponents to err, or drive them back from the net.

Item No. 1 on your mental check list as you await service should be the opposing netman. How close to the net
does he play? Is he always alert? (Most netmen doze off

occasionally.) Does he like to poach? An effective poacher will be playing closer to the net than the partner of a server normally would. You will have better luck returning service during the match if you can keep the net-

man honest, keep him from poaching. If you see he is playing to poach—that is, playing close to the net—a few effective lobs over his head will convey the message to him. You may have to repeat the lesson during the course of the match.

Another method is to hit the ball at him a time or two early in the match, keeping it low so that hopefully he cannot put it away if he does return it. Hitting it "at him" can take a number of variations, and the choice is yours to make, depending upon your evaluation of the intelligence, alertness, and volleying ability of the opposing netman. You can hit it directly at him; you can try to pass him down the line; or you can try to crease the right profile of his body, hitting as close to the top of the net as possible. In other words, aim approximately at the right

elbow. Hit from the correct position, this can be an effective service return. If you will imagine a ball coming at you aimed at that spot, you will see that you must move rapidly and step some distance back or away from the ball to be able to hit it cleanly. Volleying a ball hit in this way, given the fact that you probably were not expecting it there in the first place, is not only difficult, but it is additionally difficult to hit such a volley decisively enough so that the receiver cannot get it.

As the service receiver, and the man who has the shot at the netman's right elbow, you were the first to know where the ball was going, and you have a greater opportunity to recover the ball should the netman return it successfully. The angles, or lack of angles, favor you. Of course, if you are able to tell your partner in advance that you are going to hit such a shot, you as a team are much better armed.

On the other hand, had you elected to try to hit past the netman down the alley (unless you were hitting from such an angle that you had an enormous advantage on the netman) you open yourself to two effective returns by him. Should your shot not be quite accurate enough to pass him, or should he anticipate it and volley it solidly: (1) he can volley sharply crosscourt into the open triangle behind your partner at the net, or (2) he can volley deep and down the alley to your extreme forehand, which may catch you off balance and at the very least force you to hit from a disadvantageous position.

Now you know how to keep the netman honest, so that in principle he is not going to poach on your return. Your job is to hit each service as described above: low, spinning, crosscourt. You are also trying to be fast enough on your feet so that you can be moving toward the net—and a strong volleying position—as you hit the return. The minute you have mastered this shot, you will realize there are a number of possibilities open to you, and your task is to measure the adroitness of your return and the effectiveness of the server's volleying or half volleying, plus your own partner's skill at the net. If you are playing good, aggressive doubles, your partner will be standing forward of the service line someplace between the center and the singles alley line on his side of the court. Your most intelligent play may be to hit to the server in such a manner that your partner can cut off any return the server

hits up, down the middle or otherwise within your partner's range. Normally this involves your hitting to the
server's backhand, or at least to the backhand side of his
body. He may have had to turn away from the net—or at
least away from his view of your partner—to hit it, and
thus will not be able to observe your partner crowding
the middle of the court. With any luck, your partner can
put it away.

When you return wide to the server's forehand, there is
a real danger if the ball is too high—the server may blow
your partner off the court. Also, if your partner has left
the alley open a little too far, a good half volleyer, partic-

ularly on a concrete or all-weather surface, can half-volley
it past him down the alley.

Of course, if the server covers your low return to his
backhand, and consistently hits low backhand volleys
that put your team in trouble, you are going to have to direct your return differently.

When both teams are crowding the net, each pushing
to get there ahead of the other, don't forget the occasional
lob. And a lob over the server's head, not just over his
partner's, is available to you. It is a much more dangerous
lob, true, since if the server anticipates it, he need only
hang back a few seconds to find himself in excellent position to cover it. But on the other hand, if you can lob
down the middle, clearing the server's partner, so that the
server has to take it on his backhand, you may find your
team in the attacking position.

As you receive in the deuce court, consider the possibility of asking your partner to play farther toward the
center line, or farther toward the sideline, if you think his
doing so will increase your advantage over the serving
team's, or reduce their advantage over you.

In doubles, even more than in singles, the breaking of a
service game—just one break—may win the set for you.

The tactics of your return in doubles may well have to
vary depending upon the playing surface. A clay surface
generally slows the ball—both the bounce of your opponent's serve and the bounce of your return—more than an
all-weather surface or grass, and more than most carpet-
ing. A fast surface should favor the server and make it
more difficult for the receiver to follow his return to the
net; he may have to take his first volley at the service line.
(Grass, incidentally, is not so much a fast-bounce surface

as it is a low-bounce surface. It is faster than clay, but it doesn't compare with concrete or the patented surfaces such as Laykold.) It is easier for the receiver to put spin on his return off a slow or clay court bounce. His racket cannot maintain contact as long with a faster ball, and to apply a spin to your return your racket must caress the ball rather than swat it.

Incidentally, keep in mind that an uneven court surface, be it grass or clay, puts a greater premium on getting to the net. You will never get a bad bounce if you don't allow the ball to hit the ground!

VIII

Receiving from the Ad Court

Your potential as a receiver in the ad court, in doubles, is completely different from that of your partner in the deuce court. The possibilities for hitting an effective, offensive return are much greater, and the strokes you will be hitting are much easier to execute, for most players. For one thing, you can counter a serve to your forehand with a drive low and down the middle, which is not a difficult shot to hit and which is, tactically, an excellent return in doubles. Down the middle is good because (1) it offers minimal opportunity for your opponent to hit an offensive shot off your return (if you had hit an angled shot to him a greater variety of angles are immediately open to *him*), and (2) it can exploit any lack of co-ordination or co-operation that exists between the two opponents. How often have you seen both players going for the same ball, resulting in hitting each other's rackets, thus precluding an effective return? Or both letting the ball go, each having assumed that the other would be taking it?

The opportunities when returning service off your forehand are so great that you may want to leave the forehand open slightly, so the server is seduced into hitting it there. In addition to the drive down the middle, you have the possibility of a soft or heavily spun angled shot hit wide into the right-hand alley of your opponent's court as previously discussed. And if you are in good position, having reached the ball early, you also have the possibility of hitting into the left-hand alley, taking the server's netman by surprise and passing him in his own alley. This can be done more readily if he has moved away from the alley as he sees his partner's serve has pulled you into the center of the court.

The chances are, of course, that most serves will come to your backhand. Before we get into the return possibilities with your backhand, let me remind you that it may be easier to run around a serve in doubles position than it is in singles. This is because the right-hand side of your court is covered by your partner, whereas in singles it is glaringly open.

But you won't be running around most serves. Most of them you will be hitting with your backhand, crosscourt, where you have a fine, relatively easy angle that hits your opponent's backhand (assuming he is right-handed). If you keep the ball low, and the angle wide, and you catch your serving opponent at his feet as he rushes to the net, you may either have scored on an error, or forced the server to volley up to your hopefully alert partner at the net. When you study it, you may be surprised at the variety of angles available to you in returning the serve from the ad court, with your backhand.

In addition to hitting sharply crosscourt, you can hit directly at the onrushing server. This may be your best shot. Seldom in tennis can you count on scoring an outright ace on return of service, unless your game is enormously stronger than your opponents. Most players, even tournament-class players, are very well satisfied if they

If you keep the ball low and the angle wide, and you catch
your serving opponent at his feet as he rushes to the net, you
may either have scored on an error or forced the server to
volley up to your hopefully alert partner at the net.

can hit a return that forces the server to volley off his shoelaces.

It is rare to be able to hit down the middle of the court off your backhand, but it is a good shot to try occasionally to keep your opponents alert. The danger is that the net-man—partner of the server—can intercept the ball and volley it away. Don't forget that you have to turn your back slightly to the net to hit the backhand properly, and this gives him the opportunity to start his lateral move-

ment without being detected by you—just a split second, but an important one. The key to effective returning often lies in your ability to judge your advantage over the

server's partner. For example, if the serve pulls you far to
the left, your opportunity to hit down the alley past the
netman will either increase or decrease, depending upon
how he reacts to his partner's serve. If he is alert and
moves into the alley once he sees that the serve pulls you
out of court, then you must forget the down-the-line possibility and either hit low and crosscourt, or lob. Often
the netman will not be that alert, and you can pop it

down the alley.

Also, if you haven't been forced too deep by the serve,
hitting the return right at the netman can occasionally be
a good shot, although this time it should bisect the profile
line of his body at the left elbow. That will minimize his

chances of hitting it into the open triangle behind your partner.

Since the aim of good doubles is attack, and since attacking is done from the net, the object in doubles is to get you and your partner to the net, and send your opponents back. You are striving to both be up or both back—in other words, to play parallel. To do otherwise in good doubles is suicide. Given this fact, you want to hit your service return as you are moving toward the net. Hit it on your way to the net. This supplies the forward movement through the ball, mentioned earlier in this book, which you need, and means you will have to use your arm less—or less violently—thus increasing your accuracy.

Also, don't forget that you want to get to the net, if possible, before the server. This means you may have to play close in—a few feet inside the baseline—to receive service, and take the serve on the rise, or at least before it reaches the top of its bounce, particularly if it is an American twist serve. Many players who have not had tournament experience, or some other athletic experience that gives them confidence in their athletic ability and helps their co-ordination, cannot take a serve early, or on the rise. If that is your case, you must stay back and hit hard drives, or heavily spinning drives that are extremely accurate, or you must resort to the defensive lob. Don't forget that the deeper you have to retreat to handle the serve, the greater the time advantage to the server's partner (at the net), who is eager to poach on your return.

If you have to lob your return you ought to warn your partner in some way, or perhaps even instruct him to stay back with you as you receive the serve.

If you and your partner are having trouble breaking an

opponent's serve, you will want to try a change in tactics —unless it is quite obvious that you are losing, because even though the tactics are incorrect, either you or your partner cannot execute the necessary shot or shots to effectuate the tactics. Actually, even then you should change tactics, since there is no point in losing when you know how to beat your opponents.

A lob is a good change of tactics in doubles. If you can lob deep in your opponents' court consistently, you may well be able to break up their offense. They will tire if they have to hit too many overhead smashes, and if they eventually resort to lobbing back, instead of trying to smash your lobs, then they have surrendered the offensive. Given a choice, you should always lob to your opponents' backhand, of course. Very few players, except the seasoned tournament players, can hit an offensive shot off a lob to their backhand; most players will have to run around a lob to their backhands, which is not only more tiring, but also leaves them out of position.

IX

When Your Partner Receives Service

In good doubles, when your partner is receiving, you normally should be standing at the net. Standing at the net in this case does not mean standing as close as you would when your partner is serving. It means standing anywhere from just inside the service line, to, say, three or four feet behind the net. Exactly where depends on the caliber of the play and relative strengths of your team and the opponents. If your opponents are too strong for you, you may not want to play at the net at all as your partner receives, but will stay back while your partner probably hits up a lob as his service return.

In good play, the most important rule for the partner of the receiver to remember as he stands at the net is to keep his eyes on the opposing netman—the partner of the server. More specifically, you should watch the served ball up until you know in what direction it is going (to your partner's forehand, or backhand); then if you look quickly back at the netman's eyes, you will be able to tell where your partner's return is going, and thus immediately redirect your vision. By that I mean that if your partner's return is crosscourt, or down the middle, the action of the netman probably will tip you off a split second in advance. And of course, his posture and direction of glance will change if your partner is hitting up a lob.

The lateral factor of your position at the net is determined by the nature and caliber of the play. You are probably playing midway between the center service line and the singles sideline. However, you should be alert to the possibility of modifying that position if it will help your partner or disconcert the opponents. Sometimes if you stand close to the center service line—which is perfectly legal—it may distract the server. When you are playing net in ad court, standing close to the center service line can influence some servers to hit away from that line, which could be an advantage to your partner.

In summation, the position of the receiver's partner in doubles can make a difference, although sometimes a subtle difference, in the outcome, and an intelligent team would do well to devote some thought and time to it.

Answers to Questions on Return of Service

1. Should the receiver's partner play at the net if his net game is woefully inadequate?

A. There should be a captain or leader on every doubles team, even one casually thrown together. The answer depends upon how inadequate the partner's net game is, and the decision should be made by the team leader.

2. When should you drop shot in returning a service, if ever?

A. This is like the famous question asked J. P. Morgan on the cost of a yacht: he said that if you have to ask the cost, you shouldn't own one. In this case, if you have to ask, don't use it.

3. If you have a weak serve, should you start the match by serving or receiving, if you win the toss?

A. You should probably elect to receive. Many players aren't adequately warmed up—at least as far as their serve is concerned—when they start the match, and you might be able to take advantage of an opponent in this condition.

4. When receiving service in doubles, in either the deuce or the ad court, what is your best-percentage return of a serve that is wide and deep?

A. In both cases, there is nothing better than a low, cross-court return.

5. What is the best-percentage return of a service down the middle in either court?

A. In both cases, there is nothing better than a low, cross-court return.

6. In doubles, returning service down the alley keeps the netman honest; when is the best time to try this?

A. In the first place, it shouldn't be tried unless you (the receiver) think the netman is going to cross and intercept your return, or unless you think he is dead on his feet and will miss a return hit at him. Otherwise, you are taking a risk. Some players return service down the alley once in the first game as a threat to keep the netman from crossing subsequently. This is a fairly obvious ploy and should probably not be tried as an automatic move, though it should certainly be tried if you have some good reason (as a result of having observed the netman) for doing so.

In general, it should be tried in two situations: (1) as a deterrent to a netman who has been crossing successfully

against you, and (2) well into the match, when play patterns have developed, and you feel that the netman's surprise, should he get to the ball, will result in his missing or mis-hitting his return. To hit down the alley when your opponent's serve has drawn you far out of the court

is risky if you are playing against an alert netman, since he will be anticipating that very return. You must be the judge of the level of alertness and sophistication of the server's partner who is at the net.

7. In doubles, if you are right-handed and playing the ad court, how can you hit an effective crosscourt return off a serve hit wide to your backhand?

A. The key to hitting such a return is to move into position quickly so that you are behind the ball or in control of it. If you are slow in getting to the ball so that you must stretch wide to hit it, you will inevitably have trouble hitting it sharply crosscourt.

8. When should the receiver lob, in doubles?

A. The object in doubles is attack. Given two relatively equally matched teams, the one that consistently gets to the net will probably win. You should only lob on return of service if your ground strokes are not enabling you and your partner to get to the net, and if you are not winning when you get there. If your ground strokes aren't helping your team take the net, then the offensive lob is something to use. Be sure to warn your partner in advance, if possible, if you want to play with him again. A short lob from you could subject him to an unpleasant blast. If you don't have a good offensive lob, and all else has failed, you can even have your partner play back on your return and lob high and to the baseline. This is a last-resort tactic to break up a team you otherwise haven't been able to penetrate, but one that can be effective. After a player hits four or five overhead smashes from the baseline in one point, his arm may be more than a little tired.

9. In singles, how can I get more depth on my returns, without reducing my accuracy?

A. If you are shorting your returns, check your body motion and weight transfer as you are hitting. Shorting can often happen when you are returning a heavily spun serve. To lengthen your returns, rather than trying a harder or more violent swing with your arm, hold the swing at its present speed, and concentrate on moving your body and your weight forward through the ball as you hit.

(These questions were asked by Ray Robinson, veteran campaigner on New York City's public courts, and Mike Holmes, holder of scores of club titles throughout eastern Massachusetts.)

The World's Top Ten

Arthur Ashe ranked the leading returners of service in the world, as of 1975, the first ranking ever published of the players' ability on return of service. In response to the author's request, Ashe ranked the players as follows (excluding himself):

No. 1: Ken Rosewall, Australia
No. 2: Jimmy Connors, U.S.A.

Group A (definitely below the top two, but above the rest of the world), in alphabetical order:

Ross Case, Australia
Rod Laver, Australia
Ray Moore, South Africa
Ilie Nastase, Romania
John Newcombe, Australia
Dennis Ralston, U.S.A.
Marty Riessen, U.S.A.
Tony Roche, Australia

With the co-operation of the United States Tennis Association, Doubleday has published the following titles in this series:

SPEED, STRENGTH, AND STAMINA: CONDITIONING FOR TENNIS, by Connie Haynes with Eve Kraft and John Conroy
Detailed descriptions of exercises for tennis players, and suggestions for keeping in shape.

TACTICS IN WOMEN'S SINGLES, DOUBLES, AND MIXED DOUBLES, by Rex Lardner
A book for women tennis players, with specific suggestions for taking advantage of opponents' weaknesses.

SINISTER TENNIS, by Peter Schwed
How to play against left-handers, and also with left-handers as doubles partners.

RETURNING THE SERVE INTELLIGENTLY, by Sterling Lord
How you can reduce errors, minimize the server's advantage, and launch your own attack.

COVERING THE COURT, by Edward T. Chase
How to be a winning court coverer and keep maximum pressure on your opponent.

FINDING AND EXPLOITING YOUR OPPONENT'S WEAKNESSES, by Rex Lardner

THE SERVE AND THE OVERHEAD SMASH, by Peter Schwed
How the intermediate player can best hit the big shots.

The following titles are in preparation:

THE HALF VOLLEY AND THE VOLLEY
GROUND STROKES
THE TENNIS PLAYER'S DIET AND FITNESS BOOK
SPECIALIZATION IN SINGLES, DOUBLES, AND MIXED DOUBLES
USTA COACHES' FAVORITE DRILLS